News Flash!

Reporting the News

Sharon Hill

Learning Media

Contents

1. From News to The News   4

2. On the Radio   10

3. In the Paper   16

4. On the Screen   23

The Life of the Story   30

Glossary   31

Index   32

1. From News to The News

What is news?

News is coming at us all the time – on the radio, in the newspapers, and on TV. A news story can be about people, events, sport, or almost anything. It can be about something that happened today, last week, or last century. But to be news, it must have something *new* to say – new information, a new opinion, or a new way of looking at things.

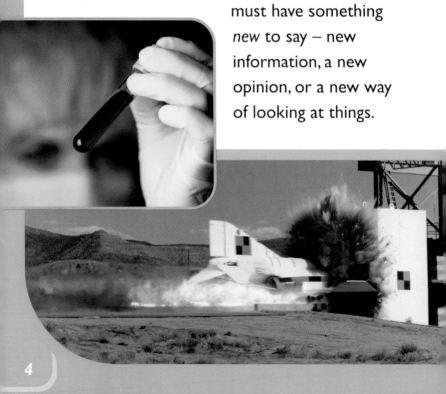

Where does news come from?

News reporters find news in many different ways. They may talk to people who have information about something that has just happened. They may get calls from people with news. Often reporters first hear about a news event or situation through a **press release**.

Creating a news story

Once a reporter gets a news **lead**, they discuss it with their **editor**. If the editor thinks that it will make a good news story, the reporter collects all the facts and they decide on an "angle."

The facts

When they are creating a news story, reporters use this checklist to make sure that they have included *all* the facts about an event or situation:

- *What* happened?
- *Who* was involved?
- *When* did it happen?
- *Why* did it happen?
- *How* did it happen?

The angle

The angle of a news story is the point of view or focus of the story. An angle helps to keep the story short and interesting. For example, for a news story about a baseball game, the angle could be that the winning team hasn't lost a game all season. Without that angle, the story might just be a boring run-by-run description of the game.

News is only new for a short time. Reporters are always working quickly so that their story will be the first one about a news event or situation. This is called "breaking news" or a "news flash."

The birth of a news story

Here's a press release that was sent to the **news media** about an oil spill. The following chapters look at how reporters, from radio, a newspaper, and television, each used it to create news stories.

Press release

A ship has spilled oil into the sea near the Poor Knights Islands, a popular fishing area and marine reserve. Rare birds and fish living there may be in danger from the oil. The ship that spilled the oil has not yet been found, but authorities are investigating.

Many news stories are reported first on radio. That's because a radio report of an event can go to air almost immediately. Television news stories have to be filmed, and newspaper stories have to be printed, so there is always a delay.

News flash

The first news report on the Poor Knights Islands oil spill was from radio reporter Lois Williams. Lois, who lives near the islands, got a phone call late at night from a **contact**.

After finding out as much as she could about the spill, Lois quickly wrote a voice script. She then phoned in her script to the radio station (even though it was the middle of the night). The news presenter read it on the next news bulletin.

" I knew it was a good news story because it was an event that a lot of people would care about. "
Lois Williams, radio reporter

Features of a radio news story

Radio news stories are short – often taking less than thirty seconds. A radio voice script needs to explain the news event as simply as possible because listeners will get only one chance to hear and understand it.

- *Lead:* the first sentence of a radio story, telling listeners what the item is about and introducing the rest of the story

- *Voice script:* the story written and recorded by the reporter

- *Sound bites:* recordings of people talking about the news event

- *Lockout:* the final words, giving the reporter's name

- *Wildtrack:* background sounds, recorded out **in the field** to make the story more realistic.

A reporter combines the voice script with the sound bites and wildtrack, and the story is ready to go **on air**.

SLUG   AUTHOR TIME (2000) MOD AUD DUR CUME   B/TIME
DU OIL SPILL WILLIAMS/Dec 03 1:45/03 1:55   0.47
INFO:
                               SUB: WILLIAMS
H/L: CONCERN OVER OIL SPILL IN NORTHLAND WATERS.

lead

Environmental agencies in Northland are on full
alert, after an oil spill near the Poor Knights
Islands.

The Northland Regional Council says the spill is
several miles across; it appears to be bilge
discharge from a ship, and it's heading for the
marine reserve, east of Whangarei. *Voice script*

Tony Phipps, of the council says the slick is
a mixture of light oil and large, tarry lumps
- and these could damge the fragile marine ecology
if they reach the Poor Knights.

He says the two ships were seen heading north,
off the east coast last night, and the Maritime
Safety Authority is investigating to see if either
is responsible for the oil spill.

Meanwhile Regional Council and Conservation staff
are preparing for the worst: they're taking out
boats at first light to assess the damage to the
marine reserve, and rescue any oiled birds.

In Whangarei, Lois Williams *lockout*

13

Follow-up stories

Over the next ten days, Lois filed several more radio stories about the oil spill. For these follow-up stories she had more time so was able to record her scripts herself in an **audio suite**.

The angles that Lois used in her radio stories were:

○ the effect of the oil on the environment and the cleanup effort

> *I rang Wade Doak, who's been diving at the Poor Knights for forty years. He was very upset at the mess the oil had left in one of his favorite spots, the Rikoriko Cave. I used a recording of him talking about the cave in one of my stories.*

○ the possibility of boats being banned from the islands

○ the identity and prosecution of the boat owner who dumped the oil.

3. In the Paper

Most newspaper stories are longer than radio or TV news stories and so can give more information. Gathering all the facts for a written news story can be a big job, especially if the story is going to press the same day.

First story: big news

Newspaper reporter Tony Gee first heard about the oil spill near the Poor Knights Islands when a contact called him.

> I knew that this was a good story because the Poor Knights Islands are one of the top places in the world for diving. I knew that an oil spill there would interest lots of people who care about the environment.

The editor of his newspaper decided that the most attention-grabbing angle would be to focus on the ship that had dumped the oil.

Tony spent a long time getting facts and quotes from people over the phone. He arranged for a photographer to take pictures of the oil spill. Once he had all the information he needed, he wrote a story and faxed it to his newspaper's **subeditor**. The subeditor decided to make it the lead story. The **lead story** needs to be big, so the subeditor combined Tony's story with one written by another reporter, Jason Collie.

To catch readers' attention, the subeditor put a photo of an oil-covered bird in the top-left corner – the part of the page where most people look first. The paper's graphic designer produced a map of the area, and the subeditor wrote a headline. The story wasn't published until the second day of the oil spill. The reason for the delay was because the newspaper comes out in the morning and reporters did not have enough time to do a story for the first day.

picture

headl

High seas hunt for oil-dump

byline

intro

By TONY

An inte for an oil Islands.
Patches kill seabi world-fam
Thick bays and on Thur
It is from a stage wide.
The uniqu plants were serva as a spot
Wad the Rike bou
all sa Au
y c li

caption

CASUALTY: Alan Fleming and other Conservation Department staff are working to save wildlife from the oil slick which washed into the Poor Knights Islands. They expect birds that congregate around the islands to continue to be caught in oil patches.

Features of a newspaper story

- *Headline:* draws attention to the story and captures reader's interest

- *Byline:* the name of the writer

- *Intro:* a summary of the story, so that the reader can decide whether they want to find out more

- *Pictures:* photographs, maps, or sketches to break up the written text and give visual information about the news event

- *Caption:* words explaining the picture

- *Quotes:* what people have said, word-for-word – backing up the story with people's direct experience of the news event.

ship

e ship believed responsible
ldlife at the Poor Knights

margarine may continue to
for several days around the
Northland's east coast.
emulsified oil have entered
nds since the slick developed

Poor Knights Islands

Tawhiti
Rahi Is

Aorangi
Island

AUCKLAND

the cave on the southern island of

ive the slick away as it broke up
workers believe oil patches will
hat congregate around the coast-
at night.
hority and the Northland Regional
ships went past the islands, 22km
will track them to their next ports to
h hat from the slick.
atio staff yesterday retrieved sea-
lso scooped up concentrated patches

e doing their best, but it was inade-
is like trying to pick up bits of coal
l huge amounts of wool to soak up the
ying no ... s between the

19

Second story: a new angle

On the fourth day of the oil spill, the wind started to blow the oil away from the Poor Knights Islands. Tony and his editor decided that this was a good angle for another story that would be very different from the first one. Tony wrote less **copy** this time and decided that a photograph wasn't needed. Because it was smaller and had a less exciting angle, the subeditor placed this story on page 4.

Po

Oil da

By TONY GEE

WHANGAREI —
Poor Knights
reserve from th
quences of Thu
"The impact
lot worse if ca
tions had com
Northland R
monitoring ma
yesterday.
"It's a tra
any oil in a n
were saved t
wind."
Regional
ment of C

NEWS

Knights saved by wind

could have been worse

decide today whether to continue cleanup work or let clumps of oil disperse naturally through wind and tides.

An inspection of the caves and bays is to be made this morning, after the major environmental scare, when large areas of floating bilge oil from a still-unidentified ship threatened marine and bird life on the islands 4km from Tutukaka off ... and east coast.

A ma... ...tion was launched ... ...to clean u... spilled so... washed a... ber of se...

on the western side of the islands.

Suspicions are focused on two ships, which will be asked to provide samples of bilge oil for comparison.

Mr Phipps said five or six more dead oil-covered birds, probably shearwaters, had been picked up from the sea during the weekend.

A smaller number of dead and injured oiled birds, including penguins and the Bullers shearwater species which nests only on the Poor Knights, were found on Friday. More dead birds are expected

the most effective cleanup method was to do it manually.

"We couldn't use skimmers or booms on the open sea in wind and we couldn't use a lot of equipment in the caves and bays on the islands."

He estimates cleanup costs so far at between $30,000 and $50,000.

Northland-based diver, marine conservationist and author Wade Doak said yesterday that the best outcome to the incident would be to become better prepared in future.

"I'm not knocking the guys working out there cleaning up. They've been doing their best but it's a matter of finding the best methodology to handle this sort of

Friday, what was happening is open to criticism. If nets and buckets are effective [in scooping up spilled oil] then it would be more effective to have more than just one or two boats doing it.

"We need someone in the country who knows all about oil spills and who has no axe to grind to come up with some strategies."

A voluntary code has existed since 1994 for oil tankers allowing captains to choose whether to go out to sea round the Poor Knights or cut between the islands and the mainland — a distance of 9 nautical miles.

Many skippers take the easier, direct route inside the Poor Knights ...uld push for these guys to ...w extra miles around the K... said Mr Doak.

The good thing about newspaper stories is that you can reread them. You usually get only one chance to see or hear the news with TV and radio news stories.

Third story: end of story

The next day, people began cleaning the oil out of coastal caves. Tony and his editor decided that this was a good angle to take for one more story. The story was about the same length as the second one but included a photograph.

The oil spill was less interesting news now, so the subeditor placed this story on page 6.

Several small articles on the spill were written later by other reporters on the paper. News about the oil spill lasted in the newspaper for about three weeks. This is longer than it lasted on both radio and TV.

4. On the Screen

Television is a very powerful way of reporting news because people can actually see things happening. TV news editors prefer stories with some action that will look interesting on the screen and those that can be filmed easily. TV stories need to be easy to follow, but they can still give a lot of information because they use pictures, sound, and text.

POORER KNIGHTS

On the spot

TV reporter Kim Hurring was on her way to work when she heard about the oil spill on the radio. So when she was asked to report on it, she already knew a bit about it. She had most of the day to do a story for the TV news program that night.

Kim called a few people who had information about the spill, then she and a camera operator went to the islands by helicopter and boat. They filmed shots of the area and the oil in the water.

Filming for TV

The camera operator tries to get many different "general" shots of the whole scene as well as closeup shots of people involved in the news event. Filming interviews requires closeups and wide shots of the person talking and some shots of the reporter. TV news stories are less than four minutes long, so only a small amount of the footage that the camera operator shoots will be used.

After talking to lots of people, Kim filmed interviews with just three of them: a person who was trying to save birds from the oil, a tourism boat operator, and a boat owner who was helping to clean up the oil. Finally, she did a piece-to-camera, which she'd written just before it was filmed. Piece-to-camera scripts are often written on the spot so that they are right up to date.

Mike Thorsen
DOC

NEWS

Back at the TV studio, Kim edited the story with the video editor in the editing suite. They put together the best shots of the island, the piece-to-camera, and the interview footage so that the whole story looked good and was easy to understand. Kim wrote and recorded a voice-over to fill in the gaps and explain the pictures.

Graphics were added, and the story was ready just in time for the evening news program. After all that effort, it was just two minutes ten seconds long, but it was important enough to be the second news item.

Features of a TV news story

 ○ *Lead-in:* the story introduced by the news presenter before it is screened
○ *Graphics:* any writing, charts, or maps

 ○ *Voice-over:* the voice speaking while the film is shown – written and recorded by the reporter, usually after the pictures have been put together

 ○ *Caption:* the words along the bottom of the screen, usually naming the person being interviewed
○ *Interview:* film footage of the reporter talking to someone about the news event

 ○ *Piece-to-camera:* the reporter talking directly to the camera about the news event, usually on the spot
○ *Sign-off:* the reporter giving their name and TV station.

Follow-up story

There was only one more TV news report on this event, the next day, which focused on the hunt for the ship that had spilled the oil. So the story had a short life on TV, compared with radio and newspapers. Kim says that you can never tell how long a story will last on TV. Some start small and grow bigger, and others start with a bang and then die away like this one did.

The Life of the Story

Media: Radio
First report: Friday morning
Life: 10 days
Reasons for life: Human interest story (about people)
Local reporter on the spot
Radio stories can be short bursts of new information

Media: Newspaper
First report: Saturday morning
Life: 3 weeks
Reasons for life: Local reporter
Human interest story (about people)
Newspaper stories are longer and can give more information

Poor Knights
Oil damage could have been

Media: TV
First report: Friday evening
Life: 2 days
Reasons for life: Reporter didn't live in the area
Action didn't last long

Glossary

(These words are printed in bold type
the first time they appear in the book.)

audio suite: the room where the audio producer
edits sound

contact: a person who calls a reporter with
breaking news

copy: the text of a news story

editor: the person who decides what goes into the
newspaper, the TV news, or the radio news and
chooses stories and angles with the reporters

footage: an amount of film or videotape

in the field: outside the studio

lead: a piece of information that might lead to a story

lead story: the most important news story, at the top
of the front page of a newspaper or the first story
on the TV or radio news

news media: organizations that publish news

on air: being broadcast on radio or television

press release: a statement given to the news media

subeditor: the person who edits a reporter's
story, writes the headline, and decides where
it will appear

Index

angle	6, 7, 15, 17, 21, 22
byline	19, 20
caption	18, 20
headline	19, 20
intro	19, 20
lead-in	28
piece-to-camera	26, 28
press release	5, 9
voice-over	27
voice script	11, 12, 13